THROUGH
MY EYES

RUBY BRIDGES

ARTICLES AND INTERVIEWS COMPILED ELL

SCHOLASTIC PRESS ◆ NEW Y

To my mama,

truly an unsung hero, for having the courage and faith to take a stand— not just for her own children but for all children;

To my teacher, Mrs. Henry,

for knowing right from wrong and for having the courage to proclaim it to the world in spite of the opposition;

To Mrs. Smith,

who gave me much and knew not that she gave at all— I was most blessed to have this lady in my life for a brief period of time;

To Bob Coles,

who in my mind is the vessel God used to keep my story alive;

To Mother,

For allowing me into her heart; for allowing me to curl up in her bed whenever I need spiritual guidance. Know that I am truly grateful for her commitment to my spiritual growth,

And in memory of my father.

LIBRARY OF CONGRESS CATALOGING-IN-PUBLICATION DATA

Bridges, Ruby. Through my eyes   p.   cm.
Summary: Ruby Bridges recounts the story of her involvement, as a six-year-old, in the integration of her school in New Orleans in 1960.
ISBN 978-0-590-18923-1 (hc)
1. Bridges, Ruby—Juvenile literature. 2. Afro-American children—Louisiana—New Orleans—Biography—Juvenile literature. 3. Afro-Americans—Louisiana—New Orleans—Biography—Juvenile literature. 4. New Orleans (La.)—Race relations—Juvenile literature. 5. School integration—Louisiana—New Orleans—Juvenile literature. [1. Bridges, Ruby. 2. Afro-Americans—Biography. 3. School integration—Louisiana—New Orleans. 4. New Orleans (La.)—Race relations.] I. Title.
F379.N59 N435 1999   379.2'63'092—dc21   [B]   98-49242   CIP

50 49 48 47 46 45 44 43 42   19 20
Printed in Malaysia   108
First edition, September 1999

The text type was set in Mrs. Eaves. Book design by Kristina Albertson

DEAR READER:

*M*ost of my life has been spent working in the world of civil rights and human rights. In that world are many stories of loss, many stories of victory, and many stories that deal with the courage of those who stand up against injustice.

Nothing can be more moving than watching a small black child climbing the steps to her elementary school that historically and legally did not welcome her presence. Ruby Bridges had been called by her country to perform an act of profound bravery—to become the black child in an all-white school.

By this simple act of courage, Ruby moved the hearts and opened the minds of millions of people. Her story was and is an inspiration. You will find this book comforting, informative, and worthy of your attention.

HARRY BELAFONTE

When I was six years old, the civil rights movement came knocking at the door. It was 1960, and history pushed in and swept me up in a whirlwind. At the time, I knew little about the racial fears and hatred in Louisiana, where I was growing up. Young children never know about racism at the start. It's we adults who teach it.

In spite of the aftereffects of the whirlwind, I feel privileged now to have been a part of the civil rights struggle. The 1950's and 60's were important decades: Negroes, as African Americans were known then, dared at last to demand equal treatment as American citizens. School integration was only one part of the struggle, but an absolutely essential part.

In 1954—coincidentally, the year I was born—the U.S. Supreme Court ordered the end of "separate but equal" education for African-American children. Because of her race, Linda Brown was not allowed to attend her local elementary school. All nine justices of the Supreme Court agreed that Linda had a legal right to go to that school. But for years afterward, the Court looked the other way when states in the South ignored its order. Black children in states like Louisiana and Mississippi continued to attend all-black public schools. White children went to separate and usually better schools.

By 1957, less than two percent of southern schools had been integrated. That year, nine black high school students enrolled in a white school in Little Rock, Arkansas. The white segregationists in Arkansas were furious. President Dwight D. Eisenhower ordered federal troops—soldiers with rifles and machine guns mounted on military jeeps—to protect the "Little Rock Nine" in their school.

Even after the events in Little Rock, Louisiana continued to ignore its African-American children. However, the civil rights

Does segregation of children in public schools solely on the basis of race, even though the physical facilities and other "tangible" factors may be equal, deprive the children of the minority group of equal education opportunities? We believe that it does. . . .To separate them from others of similar age and qualifications solely because of their race generates a feeling of inferiority as to their status in the community that may affect their hearts and minds in a way unlikely ever to be undone.

—*Brown v Board of Education of Topeka, Kansas*

movement was growing stronger. A federal court gave the city a deadline for school integration: September 1960.

I don't remember everything about that school year, but there are events and feelings I will never forget. In writing this book, I recall how integration looked to me then, when I was six and limited to my own small world. However, as an adult, I wanted to fill in some of the blanks about what was a serious racial crisis in the American South. I have tried to give you the bigger picture—through my eyes.

The National Guard escorted the Little Rock Nine to school to protect the students from angry segregationists.

I came into this world as a healthy, seven-pound baby, my parents' first child, on September 8, 1954. From the small hospital in Tylertown, Mississippi, where I was born, my mother took me home to the farm where my parents lived with my father's family.

My father's parents were sharecroppers who worked the land under the broiling Mississippi sun. Sharecroppers didn't own the land they farmed. They paid rent to the landowner in whatever crops they raised and struggled to survive on what was left.

My mother's parents were Mississippi sharecroppers, too. When I was older, I loved visiting the farm where they lived. After my family moved to New Orleans, I went back and spent every summer of my childhood on that vegetable and dairy farm. I wasn't the only child on the farm. My mother came from a big family, and many cousins went to help out in the summer. My parents stayed in New Orleans to work.

My grandfather tended the dairy herd while my grandmother Amy took charge of the two acres of vegetables. You can grow a lot of vegetables on two acres. All summer long, my grandmother organized my cousins and me into work shifts, heading into the fields to pick beans or cucumbers or helping in the kitchen with the cooking and canning. Canning meant preserving food so that every family would have vegetables through the winter. That was how the grown-ups fed us children.

Those hot summers were good ones. When I fell into bed at night I was tired, yet happier than at any other time of my life. I took the summers for granted then, the way kids do, but I know now they were a gift. Best of all was being with my grandmother and being one of her favorites. Her love and attention made me feel very special then—and even more so now.

PICKING COTTON WAS HARD
WORK THAT PAID LITTLE.

Sharecropping is hard work. On the day before Ruby was born, I carried 90 pounds of cotton on my back. I wanted a better life for Ruby.

—LUCILLE BRIDGES, RUBY'S MOTHER

My family moved to the old seaport city of New Orleans in 1958, when I was four. On the block where I lived, everyone was black. White families lived on the next block, but at the time, it seemed as if they were a world apart. A lot of the black people, like my parents, had left farms in Louisiana or Mississippi to make a better living in the city.

In New Orleans, we rented the front part of a large house on France Street. It was a big rooming house, with other families living in apartments upstairs and in the back. Our part of the house had only two bedrooms, so my younger brothers and my sister and I shared a room. In 1960, when I started first grade, there were four Bridges children, but eventually there were eight of us piling into bunk beds in that bedroom.

The best part of the house was the kitchen, where we ate all our meals. My mother did a lot of cooking. We had big southern breakfasts, with grits, bacon and eggs, and homemade biscuits. At night, my mother sometimes cooked New Orleans-style food, like red beans and rice or fried catfish or shrimp. For dessert, she sometimes made one of my favorites—banana pudding or sweet potato pie.

The weather in New Orleans never gets too cold, so we played outside most of the year. We stayed close to home and never left the block. Most afternoons, my mother wanted me to keep an eye on my brothers and sister, but I managed to play jacks and jump rope with my friends and climb the huge China ball tree by the house. On the weekends, somebody was always starting up a softball game in the lot next door. My world in those days was comfortable and safe.

My parents didn't have much education, and it took everything they had to keep the family going. My father worked as a service station attendant. My mother sometimes took night jobs, like cleaning rooms in one of the city's hotels. I remember my mother taking a job making caskets. She would tell stories about how

NEW ORLEANS IS THE HOME OF THE FAMOUS MARDI GRAS PARADE.

she and the other workers would get into the caskets to see if they were comfortable and how they would take naps in the caskets during their breaks. My brothers and sister and I thought those stories were fascinating.

My mother brought us up to believe that God is always there to protect us. She taught us there is a power we can pray to anytime, anyplace.

At the same time, my mother didn't allow any nonsense from her children. She was strict. We all had chores and were expected to carry them out. When she told us to do something, we were supposed to say, "Yes, m'am," and not too much else about it.

When it was time for me to start kindergarten, I went to the Johnson Lockett Elementary School. My segregated school was fairly far from my house, but I had lots of company for the long walk. All the kids on my block went to Johnson Lockett. I loved school that year, and my teacher, Mrs. King, was warm and encouraging. She was black, as all the teachers in black schools were back then. Mrs. King was quite old, and she reminded me of my grandmother.

What I didn't know in kindergarten was that a federal court in New Orleans was about to force two white public schools to admit black students. The plan was to integrate only the first grade for that year. Then, every year after that, the incoming first grade would also be integrated.

In the late spring of my year at Johnson Lockett, the city school board began testing black kindergartners. They wanted to find out

MANY AMERICANS—BLACK AND WHITE—GATHERED TOGETHER IN CIVIL RIGHTS DEMONSTRATIONS TO SHOW THAT THEY WANTED INTEGRATION AND EQUAL OPPORTUNITIES FOR ALL.

which children should be sent to the white schools. I took the test. I was only five, and I'm sure I didn't have any idea why I was taking it. Still, I remember that day. I remember getting dressed up and riding uptown on the bus with my mother, and sitting in an enormous room in the school board building along with about a hundred other black kids, all waiting to be tested.

Apparently the test was difficult, and I've been told that it was set up so that kids would have a hard time passing. If all the black children had failed, the white school board might have had a way to keep the schools segregated for a while longer.

That summer, my parents were contacted by the National Association for the Advancement of Colored People (NAACP). The NAACP is an old and well-respected civil rights organization. Its members work to get equal rights for black people.

Then there were the long and continuing series of research reports showing that Blacks scored lower on IQ tests than Whites, without acknowledging that the tests were standardized on, and culturally biased in favor of, White middle-class children.
—ROBERT-JAY GREEN, "RACE AND THE FIELD OF FAMILY THERAPY"

Several people from the NAACP came to the house in the summer. They told my parents that I was one of just a few black children to pass the school board test, and that I had been chosen to attend one of the white schools, William Frantz Public School. They said it was a better school and closer to my home than the one I had been attending. They said I had the right to go to the closest school in my district. They pressured my parents and made a lot of promises. They said my going to William Frantz would help me, my brothers, my sister, and other black children in the future. We would receive a better education, which would give us better opportunities as adults.

My parents argued about what to do. My father, Abon, didn't want any part of school integration. He was a gentle man and feared that angry segregationists might hurt his family. Having fought in the Korean War, he experienced segregation on the battlefield, where he risked his life for his country. He didn't think that things would ever change. He didn't think I would ever be treated as an equal.

Lucille, my mother, was convinced that no harm would come to us. She thought that the opportunity for me to get the best education possible was worth the risk, and she finally convinced my father.

Ruby was special. I wanted her to have a good education so she could get a good job when she grew up. But Ruby's father thought his child shouldn't go where she wasn't wanted.

There were things I didn't understand. I didn't know Ruby would be the only black child in the school. I didn't know how bad things would get.

I remember being afraid on the first day Ruby went to the Frantz school, when I came home and turned on the TV set and I realized that, at that moment, the whole world was watching my baby and talking about her.

At that moment, I was most afraid.

—LUCILLE BRIDGES

When September came that year, I didn't start first grade at William Frantz. The lawmakers in the state capital, Baton Rouge, had found a way to slow down integration, so I was sent back to my old school. I didn't know I was ever supposed to go to school anywhere else, so being back at Johnson Lockett was fine with me.

All through the summer and early fall, the state legislators fought the federal court. They passed twenty-eight new anti-integration laws.

CHILDREN ENTERING WILLIAM FRANTZ PUBLIC SCHOOL

They even tried to take over the public school system. The Louisiana governor, Jimmie H. Davis, supported the segregationists. He said he would go to jail before he would allow black children in white schools. He even threatened to close all of the public schools rather than see them integrated.

The federal court, led by Federal District Court Judge J. Skelly Wright, unyielding in his commitment to upholding the law of the land and in his dedication to equal opportunity for all Americans, would block the segregationists again and again. J. Skelly Wright struck down the state's new anti-integration laws as unconstitutional. School integration would proceed. Praise the Lord!

The judge couldn't enforce his order in time for the start of school in September, but he set a new deadline for Monday, November 14.

The anger all across New Orleans convinced

Judge Wright that things might grow violent. He asked the U.S. government to rush federal marshals to New Orleans to protect the black first graders.

There were four of us in all. There was a fifth girl originally, but her parents decided at the last minute not to transfer her. Three of the remaining children, all girls, were to go to a school named McDonogh. I was the fourth child. I was going to integrate William Frantz Public School, and I was going alone.

On Sunday, November 13, my mother told me I would start at a new school the next day. She hinted there could be something unusual about it, but she didn't explain. "There might be a lot of people outside the school," she said. "But you don't need to be afraid. I'll be with you."

All I remember thinking that night was that I wouldn't be going to school with my friends anymore, and I wasn't happy about that.

FOR SEGREGATION: JIMMIE H. DAVIS, THEN GOVERNOR OF LOUISIANA, THREATENED TO CLOSE THE PUBLIC SCHOOLS RATHER THAN INTEGRATE THEM.

FOR INTEGRATION: J. SKELLY WRIGHT, UNITED STATES DISTRICT JUDGE, WAS DEDICATED TO EQUAL OPPORTUNITY FOR ALL AMERICANS; HE BLOCKED THE SEGREGATIONISTS AGAIN AND AGAIN.

Five Negro girls are scheduled to enter the first grades of two white schools here [New Orleans] Monday. This would mark the first step toward integration below the college level in any of the five resisting states of the Deep South. They are South Carolina, Georgia, Alabama, Mississippi, and Louisiana.

—*THE NEW YORK TIMES*, NOVEMBER 11, 1960

My mother took special care getting me ready for school. When somebody knocked on my door that morning, my mother expected to see people from the NAACP. Instead, she saw four serious-looking white men, dressed in suits and wearing armbands. They were U.S. federal marshals. They had come to drive us to school and stay with us all day. I learned later they were carrying guns.

I remember climbing into the back seat of the marshals' car with my mother, but I don't remember feeling frightened. William Frantz Public School was only five blocks away, so one of the marshals in the front seat told my mother right away what we should do when we got there.

"Let us get out of the car first," the marshal said. "Then you'll get out, and the four of us will surround you and your daughter. We'll walk up to the door together. Just walk straight ahead, and don't look back."

When we were near the school, my mother said, "Ruby, I want you to behave yourself today and do what the marshals say."

We drove down North Galvez Street to the point where it crosses Alvar. I remember

POLICE OFFICERS AND FEDERAL MARSHALS SURROUNDED WILLIAM FRANTZ AND McDONOGH (SHOWN HERE) PUBLIC SCHOOLS.

looking out of the car as we pulled up to the Frantz school. There were barricades and people shouting and policemen everywhere. I thought maybe it was Mardi Gras, the carnival that takes place in New Orleans every year. Mardi Gras was always noisy.

As we walked through the crowd, I didn't see any faces. I guess that's because I wasn't very tall and I was surrounded by the marshals. People yelled and threw things. I could see the school building, and it looked bigger and nicer than my old school. When we climbed the high steps to the front door, there were policemen in uniforms at the top. The policemen at the door and the crowd behind us made me think this was an important place.

It must be college, I thought to myself.

ACROSS THE STREET FROM THE SCHOOL, POLICE KEPT AN EYE ON ANGRY DEMONSTRATORS.

[Nov.14]

Today, hundreds of city policemen began to assemble in the mixed white and Negro residential districts of the two schools as the sun burned away the haze from the Mississippi River.

Black squad cars cruised slowly through the narrow streets between modest white frame dwellings set among palms, oleanders, and crepe myrtle. Patrolmen in gold-striped uniforms, black boots, and white crash helmets dismounted from motorcycles to direct traffic. Police officials and detectives stationed themselves around the school buildings and inside the halls. Deputy federal marshals wearing yellow armbands made a final check and drove to the homes of the four pupils. . . .

Some 150 whites, mostly housewives and teenage youths, clustered along the sidewalks across from the William Frantz School when pupils marched in at 8:40 a.m. One youth chanted, "Two, four, six, eight, we don't want to integrate; eight, six, four, two, we don't want a chigeroo."

Forty minutes later, four deputy marshals arrived with a little Negro girl and her mother. They walked hurriedly up the steps and into the yellow brick building while onlookers jeered and shouted taunts.

The girl, dressed in a stiffly starched white dress with a white ribbon in her hair, gripped her mother's hand tightly and glanced apprehensively toward the crowd.

—*THE NEW YORK TIMES*, NOVEMBER 15, 1960

There was almost a carnival atmosphere on Alvar Street, outside the school. Women in bright, tight toreador pants, their hair done up in curlers, struck poses in front of the press cameras, kidding policemen and reporters. Children, waving Confederate flags, dashed up and down the street grabbing coffee from a truck that displayed a sign: "For white mothers only."

—GOOD HOUSEKEEPING, APRIL 1962

Once we were inside the building, the marshals walked us up a flight of stairs. The school office was at the top. My mother and I went in and were told to sit in the principal's office. The marshals sat outside. There were windows in the room where we waited. That meant everybody passing by could see us. I remember noticing everyone was white.

All day long, white parents rushed into the office. They were upset. They were arguing and pointing at us. When they took their children to school that morning, the parents hadn't been sure whether William Frantz would be integrated that day or not. After my mother and I arrived, they ran into classrooms and dragged their children out of the school. From behind the windows in the office, all I saw was confusion. I told myself that this must be the way it is in a big school.

That whole first day, my mother and I just sat and waited. We didn't talk to anybody. I remember watching a big, round clock on the wall. When it was 3:00 and time to go home, I was glad. I had thought my new school would be hard, but the first day was easy.

LEAVING WILLIAM FRANTZ AFTER THE FIRST DAY OF SCHOOL

A procession of mothers moved in and out of the schools, removing books and other belongings of their children. Many vowed that their children would not return to class so long as the Negroes were there.

—*THE NEW YORK TIMES*, NOVEMBER 16, 1960

When the Negroes entered the schools, many white pupils walked out. They were encouraged by the State legislature, which passed a resolution calling for a boycott of mixed schools.

—*U.S. NEWS & WORLD REPORT*, NOVEMBER 28, 1960

When we left school that first day, the crowd outside was even bigger and louder than it had been in the morning. There were reporters and film cameras and people everywhere. I guess the police couldn't keep them behind the barricades. It seemed to take us a long time to get to the marshals' car.

Later on I learned there had been protestors in front of the two integrated schools the whole day. They wanted to be sure white parents would boycott the school and not let their children attend. Groups of high school boys, joining the protestors, paraded up and down the street and sang new verses to old hymns. Their favorite was "Battle Hymn of the Republic," in which they changed the chorus to "Glory, glory, segregation, the South will rise again." Many of the boys carried signs and said awful things, but most of all I remember seeing a black doll in a coffin, which frightened me more than anything else.

After the first day, I was glad to get home. I wanted to change my clothes and go outside to find my friends. My mother wasn't too worried about me because the police had set up barricades at each end of the block. Only local residents were allowed on our street. That afternoon, I taught a friend the chant I had learned: "Two, four, six, eight, we don't want to integrate." My friend and I didn't know what the words meant, but we would jump rope to it every day after school.

My father heard about the trouble at school. That night when he came home from work, he said I was his "brave little Ruby."

DEMONSTRATORS OUTSIDE THE SCHOOL CARRIED CONFEDERATE FLAGS, POSTERS, AND A BLACK DOLL IN A COFFIN, A TERRIFYING IMAGE.

Leaving the school each day seemed even more frightening than arriving in the morning.

I always drove to work and kept my car on the playground behind the school building. The police had turned the playground into a parking lot because it was the only area they could protect.

On leaving school in the afternoon—even with a police escort—you were always fearful of how the people gathered along the sidewalks might choose to protest that day as you drove past them. The New Orleans police were supposed to be there to help us, but they very much disliked being the ones to enforce integration, so you never could be confident of their support and cooperation.

—BARBARA HENRY, RUBY'S FIRST-GRADE TEACHER

On the second day, my mother and I drove to school with the marshals. The crowd outside the building was ready. Racists spat at us and shouted things like "Go home, nigger," and "No niggers allowed here." One woman screamed at me, "I'm going to poison you. I'll find a way." She made the same threat every morning.

I tried not to pay attention. When we finally got into the building, my new teacher was there to meet us. Her name was Mrs. Henry. She was young and white. I had not spent time with a white person before, so I was uneasy at first. Mrs. Henry led us upstairs to the second floor. As we went up, we hardly saw anyone else in the building. The white students were not coming to class. The halls were so quiet, I could hear the noise the marshals' shoes made on the shiny hardwood floors.

Mrs. Henry took us into a classroom and said to have a seat. When I looked around, the room was empty. There were rows of desks, but no children. I thought we were too early, but Mrs. Henry said we were right on time. My mother sat down at the back of the room. I took a seat up front, and Mrs. Henry began to teach.

I spent the whole first day with Mrs. Henry in the classroom. I wasn't allowed to have lunch in the cafeteria or go outside for recess, so we just stayed in our room. The marshals sat outside. If I had to go to the bathroom, the marshals walked me down the hall.

My mother sat in the classroom that day, but not the next. When the marshals came to the house on Wednesday morning, my mother said, "Ruby, I can't go to school with you today, but don't be afraid. The marshals will take care of you. Be good now, and don't cry."

I started to cry anyway, but before I knew it, I was off to school by myself.

At the blackboard
with Mrs. Henry

There was a certain shyness about Ruby. She would appear at the door of our room in the morning and walk in slowly, taking little steps. I would always greet her with a compliment about how nicely she was dressed to help make her feel special, as she was, and to make her feel more welcome and comfortable. We would hug, and then we would sit down side by side. We had our corner of the room, and it was cozy. I never sat in the front of the classroom apart from her. If I went to the blackboard, she was always right there with me.

I grew to love Ruby and to be awed by her. It was an ugly world outside, but I tried to make our world together as normal as possible. Neither one of us ever missed a day. It was important to keep going.

—BARBARA HENRY

The author John Steinbeck was driving through New Orleans with his dog, Charley, when he heard about the racist crowds that gathered outside the Frantz school each morning to protest its integration. He decided to go see what was happening.

He especially wanted to see a group of women who came to scream at me and at the few white children who crossed the picket lines and went to school. (At the time, I didn't know that there were other children in the building. We were kept apart.) The women were known as the Cheerleaders, and their foul language even shocked a man as worldly as Steinbeck.

I never met John Steinbeck, but he seemed to sympathize with what I was going through. He wrote about me in a book called *Travels with Charley*. Steinbeck left his dog and his truck in a parking lot. He didn't want to take them to Frantz, where his dog could get hurt or his car could get damaged. Instead he took a cab. Fearing that protestors would wreck his car, the driver didn't take Steinbeck all the way to the school, but left him a few blocks away.

Steinbeck never knew my name. My name and the names of the girls at the McDonogh school were never mentioned on television or in the newspapers. The press tried to protect us.

JOHN STEINBECK, AUTHOR OF *THE GRAPES OF WRATH* AND *THE RED PONY*, WON THE NOBEL PRIZE FOR LITERATURE.

THE ARTIST NORMAN ROCKWELL WAS INSPIRED BY PARAGRAPHS IN *TRAVELS WITH CHARLEY* TO PAINT A PICTURE CALLED *THE PROBLEM WE ALL LIVE WITH*. IT WAS PUBLISHED IN THE JANUARY 14, 1964, ISSUE OF *LOOK* MAGAZINE.

The show opened on time. Sound of sirens. Motorcycle cops. Then two big black cars filled with big men in blond felt hats pulled up in front of the school. The crowd seemed to hold its breath. Four big marshals got out of each car and from somewhere in the automobiles they extracted the littlest Negro girl you ever saw, dressed in shining starchy white, with new white shoes on feet so little they were almost round. Her face and little legs were very black against the white.

The big marshals stood her on the curb and a jangle of jeering shrieks went up from behind the barricades. The little girl did not look at the howling crowd but from the side the whites of her eyes showed like those of a frightened fawn. The men turned her around like a doll, and then the strange procession moved up the broad walk toward the school, and the child was even more a mite because the men were so big. Then the girl made a curious hop, and I think I know what it was. I think in her whole life she had not gone ten steps without skipping, but now in the middle of her first skip, the weight bore her down and her little round feet took measured, reluctant steps between the tall guards. Slowly they climbed the steps and entered the school.

— JOHN STEINBECK, *TRAVELS WITH CHARLEY*

At the start of school integration, many white parents were afraid of the protestors in front of the Frantz school. Even if the parents believed in integration, they didn't want to put their children in danger by sending them to class. However, a few families took the risk. As a Methodist minister, Reverend Lloyd Foreman was convinced that integration was morally and spiritually right and was determined to keep his daughter, Pam, in the Frantz school. That November, the minister walked Pam to and from school every day. Very quickly, the chorus of racists became obsessed with the Foremans. They taunted them without mercy.

POLICE KEEPING HECKLERS AWAY AS THE REVEREND LLOYD FOREMAN TOOK HIS DAUGHTER TO SCHOOL

The crowd was waiting for the white man who dared to bring his white child to school. And here he came along the guarded walk, a tall man dressed in light gray, leading his frightened child by the hand. His body was tensed as a strong leaf spring drawn to the breaking strain; his face was grave and gray, and his eyes were on the ground immediately ahead of him. The muscles of his cheeks stood out from clenched jaws, a man afraid who by his will held his fears in check as a great rider directs a panicked horse.

A shrill, grating voice rang out. The yelling was not in chorus. Each took a turn and at the end of each the crowd broke into howls and roars and whistles of applause. This is what they had come to see and hear.

No newspaper had printed the words these women shouted. It was indicated that they were indelicate, some even said obscene. On television the sound track was made to blur or had crowd noises cut in to cover. But now I heard the words, bestial and filthy and degenerate.

— JOHN STEINBECK, *TRAVELS WITH CHARLEY*

WOMAN THREATENING TO STRANGLE THE REVEREND FOREMAN WITH HER SCARF

The Gabrielles were another brave family. Daisy and her husband, Jim, had several children, including a six-year-old named Yolanda. Mrs. Gabrielle had been in the army during World War II, and she refused to be bullied by the protestors. When I entered William Frantz, Daisy Gabrielle did not take Yolanda out of school.

I don't remember ever seeing Yolanda, even though she was a first grader. The school building was large, and any white children who attended were kept far from my classroom. They were assigned separate teachers and were hurried in and out of school through a back entrance.

Yolanda Gabrielle came to school every day for three weeks. During that time, her family's home was attacked. Stones and rotten eggs were thrown. Windows were broken. Hecklers gathered in front of the house and threatened to hurt the Gabrielle children. Daisy's husband was about to lose his job. Though the police set up protection for the family, and a wonderful New Orleans woman named Betty Wisdom offered to drive Yolanda to school each day, Daisy Gabrielle knew her daughter was still at risk.

In the end the Gabrielles gave up. They not only took Yolanda out of school but also moved the family to another state, a northern state where Daisy's husband had grown up. It was time to get away from Louisiana.

YOLANDA AND HER MOTHER DAISY GABRIELLE, ESCORTED BY A DETECTIVE, WALKING PAST A JEERING CROWD. SHORTLY BEFORE THIS PICTURE WAS TAKEN, A ROCK HAD SHATTERED THE WINDOW OF THE CAR THEY WERE IN.

Then one afternoon, after the police had taken them through the mob, the child had looked behind her and suddenly became aware of the danger. That night she woke up screaming. When Daisy went to her, she was babbling about "those ugly ladies; those ladies who yell so ugly." Then Yolanda said her stomach hurt, that she didn't want to go to school the next day.

Daisy held her in her arms, promising she could stay home, her heart heavy with the burden she had put on her family.

—GOOD HOUSEKEEPING MAGAZINE, APRIL 1962

While I was attending William Frantz, a couple of miles away, three black girls were integrating McDonogh No. 19. Their names were Leona, Tessie, and Gail.

OPPOSITE: CROWDS WATCHING A GIRL ENTERING HER SCHOOL

THREE GIRLS (ONE HIDDEN BEHIND A MARSHAL) LEAVING MCDONOGH ELEMENTARY SCHOOL

Some thirty minutes after the scheduled start of classes the marshals pulled up at McDonogh No. 19 with three pupils accompanied by parents, a man and two women.

An angry roar went up from the whites among the mixed crowd of spectators. "Kill them niggers!" shouted one man.

The police rapidly moved the crowd off the sidewalk to a parkway in the middle of the street.

The parents and the pupils, who were in pigtails and freshly laundered dresses, were rushed into the stucco building by the deputy marshals.

—THE NEW YORK TIMES, NOVEMBER 15, 1960

Attendance dwindled until on November 17 three Negro girls and one white child were the only pupils present at McDonogh School No. 19, which normally has 467 pupils. The other "integrated" Negro had the company of only three white children in William T. Frantz School, which normally has 576 pupils.

—U.S. NEWS & WORLD REPORT, NOVEMBER 28, 1960

In those first tense days of integration, people didn't protest just in front of the schools. Trouble broke out across the city. As I sat quietly huddled with Mrs. Henry, mobs of protestors roamed the streets. People threw rocks and bricks at passing cars. Some even tossed flaming bottles of gasoline. Hospital emergency rooms began to fill up. White people drove through the city at night, leaving burning crosses as warnings in black neighborhoods. African Americans knew this was meant to frighten them into giving up integration. The segregationist organization known as the Ku Klux Klan had been burning crosses in front of black homes for many years all over the South.

White parents from New Orleans even traveled to Baton Rouge to protest school integration in front of the state legislature. They wanted J. Skelly Wright, the federal judge who ordered integration, to be removed from office.

THREE HOODED MEMBERS OF THE KU KLUX KLAN STANDING NEXT TO A BURNING CROSS AT A SATURDAY NIGHT RALLY

Parents and children from integrated New Orleans schools bore a miniature black coffin, containing a blackened effigy of U.S. Judge J. Skelly Wright, into the Louisiana Capitol. . . .

The House stood up and, with a long roll of applause, saluted the parents. . . . As the demonstrators moved into the legislative chambers, one woman in the group shouted, "The judge is dead, we have slaughtered him."

Some of the group feigned weeping and mourning, others laughed.

The blackened doll inside the yard-long coffin wore a black suit. In its pocket was a small gavel.

—NEW ORLEANS TIMES PICAYUNE, NOV. 24, 1960

*I*n the first week of school integration, the tension in New Orleans seemed to build each day. Rioters on the streets were looking for trouble. Whites assaulted blacks in broad daylight, and blacks fought back, even though the NAACP urged them not to. Vandals broke store windows and took what they could.

To curb the crowds that gathered, extra police on horseback and motorcycles were brought in. When Mayor deLesseps S. Morrison appeared on television and called for calm, militant segregationists were enraged. They felt the mayor had betrayed them.

Finally, the protests began to die down. By the end of the week, the worst of the street riots were over. Thanksgiving was coming, and the public schools were closing for a week-long holiday. City School Superintendent James F. Redmond made it clear that school integration would continue after Thanksgiving. However, resentful white parents promised not to give up. They would protest again as soon as the schools reopened.

The New Orleans school board appealed to the federal court for a temporary halt to integration. The board said it needed time to settle certain legal questions. Thurgood Marshall, the NAACP lawyer who commented on the appeal, would eventually become a justice of the United States Supreme Court.

THURGOOD MARSHALL, LAWYER FOR THE NAACP

Thurgood Marshall, counsel for the National Association for the Advancement of Colored People, opposed any suspension of desegregation.

"I don't think there's any amount of time that's going to bring any cooperation from the Legislature or the officials of Louisiana," he said.

—*THE NEW YORK TIMES, NOVEMBER 19, 1960*

On November 16, teenagers gathered outside City Hall to protest the integration of New Orleans schools.

$\mathcal{E}$verybody was glad for time out at Thanksgiving, including me. Even so, the stress didn't go away completely. The owners of the small grocery store at the end of the block suddenly told my family to stay away. Because we were a part of school integration, the white owners no longer wanted our business.

My grandparents telephoned from Mississippi to say they were afraid for us. They thought my father would be lynched—murdered by a lawless mob.

My parents didn't tell us if they were afraid for their lives, but I knew my father was worried about how to make a living. The garage where he worked had fired him because I was going to a white school.

Financial help was on its way, fortunately, and it came through the U.S. mail. People from around the country sent gifts and money. They knew what was happening in New Orleans because of television news programs, as well as magazine and newspaper articles. Many

Time out for Thanksgiving

Americans wanted to encourage us. The money made a big difference to my family, and it kept coming for months.

Along with the money came presents for me. There were toys, books, and clothes for school. The packages were addressed to me, so I thought they should be mine. My mother didn't agree. She would say, "Ruby, you have to share these things with your brothers and sister. They can't all be for you."

When one child in a family is receiving a lot of attention, it can cause problems. The gifts were wonderful, but they sometimes meant a tug-of-war. I thought my mother was being mean when she told me that I had to give some of my presents away.

We received stacks of encouraging cards and letters. Even Eleanor Roosevelt wrote me a note. She was the widow of Franklin Roosevelt, the former president of the United States. Mrs. Roosevelt's note was my mother's favorite, and she looked at it again and again.

Eventually letters came from around the world. We kept a lot of them, but they didn't survive. In 1965, a huge hurricane named Betsy flooded parts of New Orleans. Mrs. Roosevelt's letter was lost in the flood, along with the Purple Heart my father received for bravery in the Korean War. Those were sad losses.

ELEANOR ROOSEVELT, FORMER FIRST LADY.

The father of the 6-year-old girl who was transferred from a Negro school to William Frantz has been discharged [from his job]. . . .

The man's employer, W. E. Smith, said: "I wouldn't have a nigger working for me with a child in a white school. Would you?"

He conceded that the Negro had been employed by him for four years and that he was a good worker. He said whites in the area had telephoned him, warning they would boycott the station if he continued to employ the man.

—THE NEW YORK TIMES, NOVEMBER 18, 1960

I will always remember how our neighbors on France Street helped us through the winter. They came by all the time to see how we were doing. They were nervous about the racial tension in the city, but they also wanted to support us. At night, they watched the house to make sure no one was prowling around.

After the Thanksgiving break, neighbors would baby-sit or help get me dressed for school in the morning. They would also watch for the marshals' car to arrive. Once I was in it, men from the neighborhood would walk behind the car, looking for signs of trouble as the car slowly left the safety of the block. One of our neighbors, who ran his own housepainting business, offered my father a job. My father didn't hesitate. He was grateful. On the spot, he began a new line of work.

In December the crowd that gathered in front of the school was smaller than before. The people who came were angry, loud militants, but the numbers were down.

On December 5, attendance at William Frantz was at eighteen, though at the time, I did not yet know that other children were in the school.

FOUR OF THE SEVENTEEN WHITE CHILDREN WHO ATTENDED WILLIAM FRANTZ ON DECEMBER 5. WHITE SEGREGATIONISTS THREW EGGS AND ROCKS AT THE CHILDREN AS THEY LEFT THE SCHOOL.

A SEGREGATIONIST THROWING AN EGG AT A CAR CARRYING SOME OF THE WHITE CHILDREN WHO ATTENDED WILLIAM FRANTZ IN DECEMBER

The legislators in Baton Rouge were still fighting school integration in the federal courts. There was a rumor they wanted to take the case all the way to the U.S. Supreme Court, but it never happened. John F. Kennedy, a liberal Democrat, had just been elected president, and segregationists in Baton Rouge knew that Washington would be less sympathetic to their cause than before.

JOHN F. KENNEDY WON THE ELECTION IN NOVEMBER AND WOULD BECOME PRESIDENT ON JANUARY 20.

Can we honestly say that it doesn't affect our security and the fight for peace when Negroes and others are denied their full constitutional rights?

—JOHN F. KENNEDY

After Christmas, my teacher and I settled into a routine. It was odd to be the only child in class, but I finally decided this was the way it was going to be here at the Frantz school. Being Mrs. Henry's only student wasn't a chore. It was fun and felt sort of special. She was more like my best friend than just an ordinary teacher. She was a loving person, and I knew she cared about me.

Mrs. Henry and I always had fun. We did everything together, reading and word puzzles, spelling and math. We sang songs and played games. Since I couldn't go outside, we pushed desks out of the way and did jumping jack exercises.

Once or twice Mrs. Henry got permission for us to walk in the school yard, but it was strange

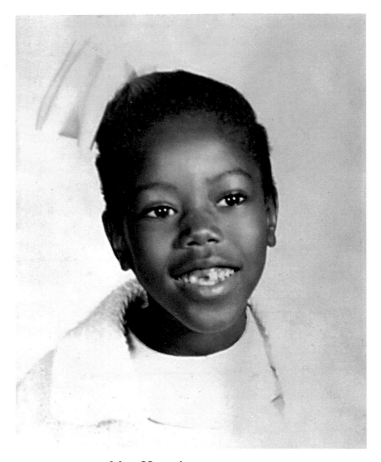

MRS. HENRY'S ONLY STUDENT

Barbara Henry

to be out there with no other kids around. I remember seeing men standing off in the corners of the yard. I thought they were hiding from somebody. Later, I learned that they were plainclothes detectives.

I spent so much time with Mrs. Henry and liked her so much that I began to speak the way she spoke. I learned later that Mrs. Henry was a northerner, from Boston, Massachusetts, and she did not have a southern drawl. I didn't sound like my brothers and sister, but I didn't know why.

I know now that Mrs. Henry influenced me a great deal that year. She had a polite, kind manner that I admired. In fact, I began to imitate her. Little by little, I grew to love Mrs. Henry. We became very attached to each other.

Ruby was a smart, sensitive person. It was a joy to go to school each day and to have her as—well—my child. I was newly married and had no children of my own at that time, and I think Ruby became "my child"! She was sweet, beautiful, and so brave. It was such an anxious time, and I often wondered how that little girl could come to school each day and be as relaxed and trusting as she was.

That year certainly wasn't the experience I thought it would be. My husband and I moved to New Orleans in September because of his job transfer. I thought New Orleans would be a romantic place, filled with southern hospitality.

I did enjoy, for a while, exploring New Orleans' historic sights as a tourist. Yet I soon longed to return to my teaching career. So one day my touring took me to the New Orleans School Headquarters to apply for a teaching position. Very soon thereafter, the Superintendent of Schools, Dr. James Redmond, phoned me and asked if I would mind teaching an integrated class. "Of course not," I answered. He then gave me the assignment at William Frantz.

Nobody at the school lifted a finger to make Ruby's life easier. The principal was a rigid, prejudiced woman who gave me no guidance or help. Ruby and I were both treated as unwelcome outsiders. When I went to the teachers' lounge at lunchtime, the other teachers at first ignored me or made unpleasant remarks about the fact that I was willing to teach a black child.

When I discovered how the other teachers were spending their time, I was appalled. Quite by accident one day, I came upon a classroom—the long-hidden other first grade—and discovered three white students talking among themselves. Their teacher, in her ankle socks and saddle shoes, was listening to the radio. Other teachers sat

ENTERING THE SCHOOL WITH
THREE U.S. MARSHALS

through the day with no students at all. They had been given the option of transferring to other schools, but they preferred a year of not-teaching.

My biggest teaching problem was that everything was so secretive. I wasn't allowed to be in contact with Ruby's family or even to know where they lived. Ruby's mother was a strong, stunning woman, and I was sorry not to be able to talk with her. I admired her courage in accepting such risks to help make a better life for Ruby and all her children.

Outside of school, I was forced to become secretive, too. My husband was in total sympathy with what I was doing, but there were very few other people who even knew where I was teaching. I didn't tell anybody because I wasn't sure who could be trusted. It was a dangerous time.

To help Ruby, I tried to explain integration more than once, but I'm not sure she understood. I told her that white people in the South had gotten used to living a certain way and that they were having trouble changing. I said people become afraid of anyone whom they think is really different from them. I wanted Ruby to know that none of the integration problem was her fault. I didn't want to allow hate to enter her life and in any way diminish her beautiful spirit. I told her she was a wonderful and special person. I told her the other children would come back to school eventually. When she asked how soon that would be, I had no answer. Ruby never complained, but I knew she was lonely.

Nowadays, when I'm invited into schools to talk about that year, I find that Ruby's story so inspires children. They feel they finally have a hero who is like them. Ruby's story allows children to feel they, too, can do very important things and they, too, can be heroes. For me, it's a pleasure to remember back. Ruby was a star. I was proud of her then, and I still am.

—BARBARA HENRY

Escorted by mother and marshals

A child psychiatrist, Robert Coles, came into my life that winter. At the time, he was a young man in the air force, stationed right outside of New Orleans. On his way to a medical conference one morning, he came upon the mob outside my school and noticed me being led into the building by the marshals. At that point, he became interested in me and wondered how I could go through such an ordeal. Soon afterward he went to the NAACP to offer his help. Dr. Coles felt that it would be easier for me to endure the stress if I had someone to talk to outside of my family.

Dr. Coles met regularly with me. He also met with the three girls from McDonogh No. 19 and with the white children from each integrated school. Every week, Dr. Coles would come to my house with his tape recorder. He would ask how I was doing, and I mostly told him I was doing fine. Then he would pull out crayons and would ask me to draw pictures of myself or the school or some of the people in my life.

Afterward we would talk about how the pictures showed what I was feeling, even if I couldn't put it into words. I think those pictures helped him to understand me.

I enjoyed the time I spent with Dr. Coles because an important man was coming to visit me and color with me, and that made me feel special. His wife was a caring person and often came to the house with him. She would always bring something special for me when she came. My mother taught Mrs. Coles how to cook gumbo, and they became good friends.

Dr. Coles later wrote about me in a number of books and articles, along with stories of other "children of crisis." He seemed to admire how well I held up through the Frantz school experience, but he was always curious about what kept me going.

CHILD PSYCHIATRIST
ROBERT COLES

GRANDFATHER

SELF-PORTRAIT, AGE 7

SELF-PORTRAIT IN SCHOOL

"I knew I was just Ruby," she told me once, in retrospect, "just Ruby trying to go to school, and worrying that I couldn't be helping my momma with the kids younger than me, like I did on the weekends and in the summer. But I guess I also knew I was the Ruby who had to do it—go into that school and stay there, no matter what those people said, standing outside. . . ."

Ruby had a will and used it to make an ethical choice; she demonstrated moral stamina; she possessed honor, courage.

—ROBERT COLES, *THE MORAL LIFE OF CHILDREN*

There were times that winter when I did show stress. Nightmares would come, and I would get up and go wake my mother for comfort.

My mother would raise herself up in bed. "Did you say your prayers before you went to sleep?" she would ask.

If I hadn't, Mama would say, "Honey, that's why you're having a bad dream. Go back now, and say your prayers."

I would do as she said, and then I would sleep. Somehow it always worked. Kneeling at the side of my bed and talking to the Lord made everything okay. My mother and our pastor always said you have to pray for your enemies and people who do you wrong, and that's what I did.

Another problem that year was lunchtime at school. I often ate in the classroom by myself while Mrs. Henry took her lunch break with the other teachers. It was a lonely time. The marshals sat outside while I opened up my lunch box. As time went on, I couldn't eat. First I blamed it on the fact that my mother fixed too many peanut butter sandwiches. Then I began to wish and wish that I could go to the cafeteria with the other children. I could smell the food they were eating.

I was convinced that the kids were there. I began hiding my uneaten sandwiches in a storage cabinet in the classroom. I poured my carton of milk into the big jar of paste we had in the room. In my magical way of thinking, not eating lunch would somehow get me to the cafeteria.

When roaches and mice began to appear in the room, a janitor discovered my old sandwiches. Mrs. Henry wasn't mad at me. She was just sorry there were so many days when I hadn't eaten. After that she usually ate with me so I wouldn't be lonely.

At home, there was a period of time when I had trouble eating, too. All I wanted were potato chips and sodas. My parents told Dr.

Poor Ruby. I felt so bad for her when we found the sandwiches. I was never going to say anything about it. For her sake, it was going to be our secret, but somehow our secret was revealed and made public. The only thing Ruby ever said to me was that she didn't like the sandwiches her mother made. I wrote to her mother, asking her to make something different.

—BARBARA HENRY

Coles about it, and he tried to talk to me. Then he remembered the woman in the crowd outside school each morning who said she was going to poison me. Dr. Coles thought I was afraid the woman really would do it.

I'm not sure if I was afraid of that or not. Perhaps I was just a picky eater. But in any case, once the year was over, my appetite returned.

There were certain treats that winter and spring that helped me feel better. One NAACP member, a woman named Mrs. Smith, was particularly good to me. She was the wife of the pediatrician I saw that year. I believe that Dr. Smith was donating his services to make sure I stayed healthy.

Mrs. Smith spent time with me to keep my

On the steps of
William Frantz at 3:00

spirits up. On the weekends, Mrs. Smith would pick me up in her car, and I would go from one world into another. I went to a zoo for the very first time and visited Storyland at City Park here in New Orleans. Mrs. Smith also took me to her home. Compared to my family, the Smiths were wealthy, and I was amazed when I saw their color television and the piano that her son gave me lessons on. The whole family was very kind to me. Those were wonderful weekends, but they left me a little dizzy and unsure about who I was and where I belonged. But now it's clear to me that those visits showed me a better side of life and made me feel that I had to do better for myself.

Near the end of the year, Mrs. Henry and I finally had company. A few white children began coming back to school, and I got an opportunity to visit with them once or twice. Even though these children were white, I still knew nothing about racism or integration. I had picked up bits and pieces over the months from being around adults and hearing them talk, but nothing was clear to me. The light dawned one day when a little white boy refused to play with me.

"I can't play with you," the boy said. "My mama said not to because you're a nigger."

At that moment, it all made sense to me. I finally realized that everything had happened because I was black. I remember feeling a little stunned. It was all about the color of my skin. I wasn't angry at the boy, because I understood. His mother had told him not to play with me, and he was obeying her. I would have done the same thing. If my mama said not to do something, I didn't do it.

The next thing I knew, it was June. That incredible year was over. Oddly enough, it ended quietly. I don't remember any special good-byes as I headed off for summer vacation. I was sorry to leave Mrs. Henry, but I somehow thought she would be my teacher again in the fall and forever.

Mrs. Henry gave me excellent grades at the end of the year, but I was told that the school principal threatened to change them. She said I had received so much individual attention that the grades weren't accurate. Mrs. Henry was angry and quarreled with the principal. Mrs. Henry was sad for me and very upset that the principal could be so mean to me. I don't know to this day whether the grades were changed or not. But it didn't matter. The principal couldn't change what was in my head.

CHILDREN TO PLAY WITH—AT LAST!

Sometime in the spring I found out three or four other first graders had been coming to the school for a while. I was stunned when I found out. It seemed cruel to keep Ruby by herself for so long. I went to the principal and told her I wanted Ruby and the other first graders to be together.

"By law, you have to integrate this school," I said. "Integration means putting black and white children in the same classroom. As I see it, you are breaking the law by keeping them separate."

The principal wouldn't budge, but I suggested we call the superintendent of schools to talk about it. The principal finally gave in. However, she would not force the other first-grade teacher to include Ruby in her class. Instead, the white children came into my classroom for part of each day.

It was progress.

—BARBARA HENRY

When I began second grade, no marshals drove me to school. In fact, they had disappeared sometime the previous spring. In the last months of first grade, a taxi driver was sent to pick me up every morning. In second grade, I was on my own.

When I went back to school in September, I expected things to be the same. On the first day, I noticed there were no protestors outside, but I went up the front steps of the building as usual and headed for my old classroom on the second floor. Then someone steered me to a different room. When I walked in, I saw at least twenty other kids. There were even a few black kids. I couldn't believe it. I was upset to learn that Mrs. Henry would no longer be my teacher. Another white teacher was in charge. I wanted to run down the hall and ask everyone I saw, "Where is Mrs. Henry?" I felt very alone again. There was no one to talk to, no one to explain things. My heart was broken.

Years later, I learned that Mrs. Henry had moved back to Boston during the summer. She was expecting her first child in the fall, and she and her husband wanted to raise their family in Boston.

For me, losing my teacher and best friend and making the change to a normal school year was very hard. No one spoke about the previous year. It was as though it had never happened. At home, there were no NAACP people coming to visit, no packages in the mail. I did see Dr. Coles sometimes, but it wasn't the same.

My second-grade teacher seemed mean to

At the end of the year, it was very hard to let go of Ruby. Even so, I wasn't sorry to leave New Orleans. Integration had been a shattering experience. After New Orleans, Boston seemed like a very appealing, uncomplicated place.

I have trouble with the word "proud," but I am pleased that Ruby and I made it through the year. A goal had been set out for Ruby, and we reached it.

For years I thought about Ruby. I had one teeny photo of her, with her front teeth missing, and I guarded it my whole life. The picture was in the top right-hand drawer of my bureau, and I would check every once in a while to make sure Ruby was still there.

She was like an invisible part of my family. Over the years, I told my children about her again and again. I had to keep the memory alive. After I left New Orleans, I knew the school was not a place where I was welcome. The principal had made it clear my association with that school was complete. I was never extended an invitation to return. But I used to wonder how Ruby was doing.

—BARBARA HENRY

SECOND GRADE BEGAN WITH NO PROTESTORS, NO MARSHALS—AND NO MRS. HENRY.

me, and she didn't seem to like me very much. She even made fun of my Boston accent when I read aloud in class.

"I know you had that northern woman for a teacher last year," she would tell me, "but you're not saying the words right."

For months, I tried to pronounce words the way the other kids did, but I never again sounded like everyone else in class. From second grade on, I felt different from the other kids in my class, and it wasn't just because of my accent. William Frantz School was integrated, but the long, strange journey had changed me forever.

There is no easy way to create a world where men and women can live together, where each has his own job and house and where all children receive as much education as their minds can absorb. But if such a world is created in our lifetime, it will be done in the United States by Negroes and white people of good will. It will be accomplished by persons who have the courage to put an end to suffering by willingly suffering themselves rather than inflict suffering upon others. It will be done by rejecting the racism, materialism, and violence that has characterized Western civilization and especially by working toward a world of brotherhood, cooperation, and peace.

—DR. MARTIN LUTHER KING, JR.

MAY 1954	Supreme Court outlaws school segregation in *Brown v Board of Education of Topeka, Kansas.*
DECEMBER 1955	Rosa Parks, a black woman, is arrested in Montgomery, Alabama, for refusing to give up her seat on a city bus to a white passenger.
SEPTEMBER 1957	President Eisenhower orders federal troops to enforce school desegregation in Little Rock, Arkansas.
FEBRUARY 1960	Four black students sit in at a "whites only" lunch counter in Greensboro, North Carolina.
NOVEMBER 1960	Four black first-grade girls integrate two public schools in New Orleans, Louisiana. Ruby Bridges is one of the first graders.
MAY 1961	Freedom Riders are attacked in Alabama while testing bus desegregation laws.
SEPTEMBER 1962	James Meredith is the first African American to enroll at the University of Mississippi.
JUNE 1963	Medgar Evers, a civil rights leader, is killed in Jackson, Mississippi.
AUGUST 1963	250,000 Americans join in the civil rights March on Washington.
1964	Martin Luther King, Jr. receives the Nobel Peace Prize.
JUNE 1964	Freedom Summer brings one thousand civil rights volunteers to Mississippi.
JULY 1964	President Johnson signs the Civil Rights Act of 1964.
MARCH 1965	The civil rights march from Selma to Montgomery, Alabama, is completed.
OCTOBER 1967	Thurgood Marshall is sworn in as the first black Supreme Court justice.
APRIL 1968	Dr. Martin Luther King, Jr., is assassinated in Memphis, Tennessee.

OPPOSITE: DR. MARTIN LUTHER KING, JR., ADDRESSING THOUSANDS OF
PEOPLE WHO WENT TO WASHINGTON, D.C., ON AUGUST 28, 1963, TO
SHOW THAT THEY SUPPORTED CIVIL RIGHTS

Maybe you'd like to know what has happened to me since I helped integrate the Frantz school. I finished William Frantz and went on to graduate from an integrated high school. I have lived in New Orleans ever since.

When I was in seventh grade, my parents separated. I think the pressure my family was under in 1960 caused serious problems in the marriage. My parents had never really agreed about my going to William Frantz, and it put a wedge between them. Money problems and other family problems continued, too, which couldn't have helped. After my parents separated, my mother moved us children out of our house on France Street and into a housing project. Over the next few years, my mother had a rough time financially. My father stayed in the old house, and I missed him so. He died of a heart attack when I was twenty-four. I wasn't a child anymore, but losing my father was terrible.

How did I get through 1960 and the long year of integration? I think it was a combination of things. For one, I really believed as a child that praying could get me through anything. I still believe that. Also, because of my mother's strict discipline, which was the way many children were raised then, I knew I was expected to obey. Getting through first grade was partly just a matter of obeying my parents. As the oldest child, I was also used to being "responsible" and looking out for my brothers and sister. The responsibility that was placed on my shoulders in first grade may have felt familiar to me, even if it was heavy. Still, I sometimes feel I lost something that year. I feel as if I lost my childhood. It seems that I have always had to deal with some adult issues.

After graduating from high school, I remember wanting to go to college. I regret not

HIGH SCHOOL GRADUATION

having that experience. My mother thought doors would automatically open for me as a result of what I had accomplished in 1960, but there was no one around to help lead me through those doors as I was led through the doors of William Frantz. After high school, I had the opportunity to study travel and tourism, and I later became a travel agent, one of the first African Americans to work for American Express in New Orleans. For fifteen years, I thoroughly enjoyed working as a travel agent. It allowed me the opportunity to see parts of the world I had only dreamed about.

Eventually I met and married a wonderful man named Malcolm Hall, and we now have four sons. We've struggled financially, but the Lord has made a way for me and my family. We have also been able to send our sons to integrated schools in a city that is less racist than it used to be.

In my adult years, I began to feel that my life should have a greater purpose. In the early

1990s, my youngest brother, Milton, was killed in a drug-related shooting in the housing project where he still lived. I was very shaken by this, as was the rest of my family. However, my brother's death woke me up in a way. It made me take a long look at my life. I slowly began to realize that what I had done in 1960 was meaningful and important. It allowed me an opportunity to speak to people and to help kids who were in trouble, the way Milton had been in trouble. Little by little, my life took on a new meaning. It's odd how misfortune can bring on new blessings.

One of the changes I made after my brother's death was to go back to the Frantz school to do volunteer work as a parent liaison. My brother's young children were students there, and I wanted to help them recover from their father's death. The school is in a poor neighborhood in the inner city, and most of the students there

RECEIVING AN HONORARY DEGREE AT THE COLLEGE OF NEW ROCHELLE

now are African American. As is true of most inner-city schools, there's never enough funding to keep William Frantz up to current standards or even to offer the students the same opportunities they would receive in some of the suburban schools I've been fortunate to visit. The kids are being segregated all over again. There aren't enough good resources available to them—and why is that?

I needed to find a way to give the William Frantz kids an equal opportunity to fulfill their hopes and dreams and enjoy school the way I did. I needed to find a way to help strengthen the school. That's what led me to establish The Ruby Bridges Foundation. To do just that. Once the foundation was funded by the proceeds from the picture book *The Story of Ruby Bridges,* by Robert Coles, we started after-school classes—just a few small classes, but it was a start. We hired teachers for multicultural arts programs. We started a ballet class, an African dance class, and a class on manners and etiquette. My hope is to bring programs like these to other inner-city schools.

I believe we must turn inner-city public schools into great schools. The Frantz school should become a great school again. All of our schools should be good enough to attract a healthy racial mix, which I believe leads to the most effective learning for everybody. If kids of different races are to grow up to live and work together in harmony, then they are going to have to begin at the beginning—in school together.

Nowadays I travel a lot, all across the country. I always feel nervous about public appearances, but I do book signings and school visits. In schools, I emphasize the importance of reading. I believe strongly in literacy and the power of education. Sometimes I also talk to kids about

RECEIVING AN HONORARY DEGREE
AT CONNECTICUT COLLEGE

race. When I'm addressing young students, I read *The Story of Ruby Bridges*. Older students whom I talk to have often seen *The Ruby Bridges Story*, the Disney television movie that was based upon my experiences. With older kids, I start a discussion about the movie or the book and then get kids talking about racial problems in their own lives. When the scary subject of race is finally broached, kids want to talk and talk. It's very satisfying.

When *The Story of Ruby Bridges* was published in 1995, I became visible again to the public, and amazing things began to happen. After the book came out, one of the people who discovered it was Barbara Henry. For many years, my first-grade teacher and I were lost to each other. When she saw the book, she was able to contact me through the publisher.

Being reunited with Mrs. Henry (as I am still tempted to call her at times) was one of the great joys of my life. We first saw each other again on a special episode of *The Oprah Winfrey Show* in 1996. We hadn't seen each other for thirty-five years. Now we not only stay in touch, but we sometimes do book signings together as well.

I have been in contact with Robert Coles again, too. He had been out of touch with me for thirty years. During that time, he published a good deal and often wrote about me, but I wasn't very aware of it. It was as though Dr. Coles was keeping my story alive until I could grow up enough to tell it myself.

To be honest, I feel as if my life grew away from me for a long time. It wasn't until I was eighteen that I even found out that the artist Norman Rockwell had made me a subject in a painting.

As a grown woman, I watched the public television series *Eyes on the Prize*, about the civil rights movement, and my mother had to point

out that some of the old film footage was of me. It's taken me a long time to own the early part of my life.

I don't know where events will go from here, but I feel carried along by something bigger than I am. For a long time, I was tempted to feel bitter about the school integration experience, not understanding why I had to go through it and go through it alone. Now I know it was meant to be that way. People are touched by the story of the black child who was so alone. Interest in the story keeps growing, and I'm not the one making it happen. The picture book and the Disney movie project seemed to fall out of the sky. I have received two honorary college degrees in recent years. I have been featured in newspaper articles and made television appearances and I've become a public speaker, a job I never would have dreamed of doing.

In all of this, I feel my part is just to trust in the Lord and step out of the way. For many years, I wasn't ready to be who I am today, but I've always tried not to lose my faith. Now I feel I'm being led by just that—faith—and now I'm closer to being at peace with myself than I ever have been.

For further information about my work and foundation, write to the following:

The Ruby Bridges Foundation
P.O. Box 127
Winnetka, Illinois
60093

SIGNING BOOKS FOR YOUNG STUDENTS AT AN EVENT HELD AT CONNECTICUT COLLEGE.

I now know that experience comes to us for
a purpose, and if we follow the guidance of
the spirit within us, we will probably find that
the purpose is a good one.

Ruby Bridges

PHOTO CREDITS:

TITLE PAGE AND PP. 14 (LEFT AND RIGHT), 24, 26, 27, 33, 34, 37, 39 (BOTTOM), 42, 49, 54, 60 (TOP), 64: AP/WIDE WORLD;
P. 46: PHOTO COURTESY OF ATLANTIC-LITTLE, BROWN; PP. 23, 40–41, 59, 60 (BOTTOM): FROM THE COLLECTION OF BARBARA
HENRY; P. 9: BLACK STAR; P. 47: DRAWINGS BY RUBY BRIDGES FROM *THE CHILDREN OF CRISIS* BY ROBERT COLES, M.D.
COPYRIGHT © 1964 BY ROBERT COLES, M.D. PUBLISHED BY LITTLE, BROWN AND CO.; P. 25: PHOTO COURTESY OF THE
NORMAN ROCKWELL MUSEUM AT STOCKBRIDGE; P. 61: PHOTO BY PAUL HORTON PHOTOGRAPHY, COURTESY OF CONNECTICUT
COLLEGE; P. 58: PHOTO BY ROGER RILEY, COURTESY OF CONNECTICUT COLLEGE; PP. 45, 51, 56, 57, 62–63:
FROM THE COLLECTION OF RUBY BRIDGES HALL; PP. 5, 10–11, 15, 21, 29, 31, 38, 39 (TOP):
UPI/CORBIS; PP. 13, 17, 19, 30, 35, 36, 53: UPI/CORBIS-BETTMANN;
P. 7: U.S. OFFICE OF EDUCATION.